Table Of Contents

Chapter 2: AI-Driven Marketing Automation Tools 1

Chapter 3: Predictive Analytics for Sales Forecasting 1

Chapter 4: Personalized AI Recommendations for E-Commerce 1

Chapter 5: AI Solutions for Human Resources and Talent Acquisition 1

Chapter 6: Data-Driven Decision-Making Tools 1

Chapter 7: Building an AI-Ready Business Culture 1

Chapter 8: Ethical Considerations and Challenges in AI 1

Chapter 9: Future Trends in AI for Small Businesses 1

Chapter 10: Resources and Tools for the AI Entrepreneur 1

Chapter 1: Introduction to AI for Entrepreneurs 2

Chapter 1: Introduction to AI for Entrepreneurs

Understanding AI and Its Relevance to Small Businesses

Artificial Intelligence (AI) has transformed the landscape of business operations, particularly for small enterprises. Understanding AI is crucial for small business owners and entrepreneurs who wish to leverage this technology to enhance efficiency and drive growth. AI encompasses a variety of algorithms and systems that can analyze data, automate tasks, and provide insights that were previously unattainable. By adopting AI-driven solutions, small businesses can optimize their processes, better understand their customers, and make informed decisions that propel them forward in a competitive market.

One of the most significant applications of AI for small businesses is in marketing automation. AI-driven marketing tools enable entrepreneurs to analyze consumer behavior, segment their audiences, and personalize marketing campaigns effectively. For instance, small businesses can use AI algorithms to predict customer preferences and tailor promotions accordingly. This level of personalization not only enhances customer engagement but also increases conversion rates, allowing small enterprises to compete with larger companies that have traditionally dominated the market.

Predictive analytics is another area where AI proves invaluable for small businesses. By leveraging historical data, predictive models can forecast sales trends and customer behaviors, enabling entrepreneurs to make proactive decisions. This capability is particularly beneficial for inventory management, as it allows small businesses to optimize stock levels based on anticipated demand. Furthermore, accurate sales forecasting can guide strategic planning, ensuring that resources are allocated efficiently and that businesses are prepared for seasonal fluctuations.

AI also plays a critical role in e-commerce, where personalized recommendations can significantly improve the shopping experience. By employing AI algorithms that analyze user behavior and preferences, small online retailers can provide tailored product suggestions. This not only enhances customer satisfaction but also drives sales by encouraging additional purchases. As more consumers turn to online shopping, small businesses that harness the power of AI to create personalized experiences will have a distinct advantage in attracting and retaining customers.

Finally, AI solutions extend to human resources and talent acquisition, where they can streamline recruitment processes and enhance employee management. For small businesses with limited HR resources, AI-driven tools can automate candidate screening, assess skill matches, and even predict employee turnover. By utilizing data-driven insights, small entrepreneurs can make better hiring decisions, foster a more engaged workforce, and ultimately drive productivity. Embracing AI in these areas not only supports operational efficiency but also positions small businesses for sustainable growth in an increasingly digital economy.

The Benefits of AI Adoption

The adoption of artificial intelligence (AI) presents numerous benefits for small business owners and entrepreneurs, particularly in enhancing operational efficiency and driving growth. By integrating AI-driven tools into their business processes, entrepreneurs can streamline operations, reduce costs, and allocate resources more effectively. Automation of routine tasks frees up valuable time, allowing business owners to focus on strategic initiatives that can propel their enterprises forward. This shift not only improves productivity but also fosters a culture of innovation, as employees can dedicate their efforts to more creative and impactful work.

In the realm of marketing, AI-driven automation tools can significantly enhance customer engagement and conversion rates. Small businesses can leverage these tools to analyze consumer behavior, segment audiences, and personalize marketing campaigns. This level of customization leads to more effective communication with potential customers, ultimately boosting sales. Moreover, AI algorithms can optimize advertising spend by identifying which channels yield the highest returns, enabling entrepreneurs to maximize their marketing budgets while minimizing waste.

Predictive analytics represents another powerful benefit of AI adoption for small enterprises. By harnessing data from various sources, entrepreneurs can forecast sales trends, understand customer preferences, and make informed inventory management decisions. This anticipatory approach not only reduces the risk of overstocking or stockouts but also helps businesses align their offerings with market demand. Consequently, entrepreneurs can enhance customer satisfaction through timely product availability and tailored service delivery, fostering loyalty and repeat business.

E-commerce platforms also stand to gain significantly from personalized AI recommendations. By analyzing user behavior and purchase history, AI can suggest products that align with individual preferences, enhancing the shopping experience. This personalization not only increases the likelihood of conversion but also encourages higher average order values as customers discover complementary products. For small businesses operating in the competitive online marketplace, these AI-driven insights can be a decisive factor in distinguishing themselves from larger competitors.

Lastly, AI solutions in human resources and talent acquisition can revolutionize how small businesses manage their workforce. By utilizing AI for recruitment processes, entrepreneurs can streamline candidate screening, identify top talent more efficiently, and reduce bias in hiring decisions. Furthermore, data-driven decision-making tools can provide insights into employee performance, enabling business owners to foster a more engaged and productive workforce. This holistic approach to human resources not only enhances operational efficiency but also contributes to a positive organizational culture, ultimately driving long-term success.

Common Misconceptions about AI

Common misconceptions about artificial intelligence often lead to misunderstandings that can hinder the potential adoption and integration of AI technologies among small business owners and entrepreneurs. One prevalent myth is that AI is only for large corporations with substantial budgets and technical expertise. In reality, many AI tools and solutions have been designed with small businesses in mind, offering accessible and affordable options that can enhance efficiency and drive growth. Entrepreneurs can leverage AI-driven marketing automation tools, predictive analytics, and personalized recommendations without the need for extensive resources or specialized knowledge.

Another common misconception is that AI will replace human jobs, causing significant unemployment. While it is true that automation may change the nature of certain jobs, AI is primarily designed to augment human capabilities rather than replace them. For small businesses, this means that AI can handle repetitive tasks, allowing employees to focus on more strategic and creative aspects of their work. By integrating AI solutions, small business owners can enhance workforce productivity and foster a more innovative work environment.

There is also a belief that AI systems are infallible and can make decisions without human intervention. This notion can lead to over-reliance on AI technologies, which may result in unforeseen consequences if those systems make errors or are fed incorrect data. It is essential for entrepreneurs to understand that AI tools should complement human decision-making rather than replace it entirely. Data-driven decision-making tools can provide valuable insights, but they require human oversight to interpret those insights effectively and align them with the broader business strategy.

Many entrepreneurs also assume that implementing AI in their operations requires extensive data and a sophisticated technological infrastructure. While it is true that data is a critical component of AI effectiveness, many AI solutions are designed to work with minimal data or can be integrated into existing systems. Small businesses can start small, using AI for specific tasks such as customer relationship management or talent acquisition, and gradually expand their AI capabilities as they become more comfortable with the technology.

Lastly, some small business owners believe that AI is a one-size-fits-all solution. The reality is that AI applications can and should be tailored to meet the unique needs of different businesses. From personalized AI recommendations for e-commerce platforms to predictive analytics for sales forecasting, entrepreneurs have a plethora of options to choose from. Understanding the specific challenges and goals of their business allows entrepreneurs to select the right AI tools that will provide the most significant impact, enabling them to harness the full potential of artificial intelligence in their entrepreneurial journey.

Chapter 2: AI-Driven Marketing Automation Tools

Overview of Marketing Automation

Marketing automation has revolutionized the way small businesses approach their promotional strategies, enabling them to operate with greater efficiency and precision. At its core, marketing automation refers to the use of software platforms and technologies to automate repetitive marketing tasks, streamline workflows, and enhance customer engagement. For small business owners, this means the ability to execute campaigns that were once reserved for larger organizations with significant marketing budgets. By leveraging marketing automation tools, entrepreneurs can create targeted campaigns, nurture leads, and analyze performance metrics without the need for extensive resources.

One of the critical advantages of marketing automation is its capability to personalize customer interactions. Modern consumers expect tailored experiences that resonate with their unique preferences and behaviors. AI-driven marketing automation tools empower small businesses to gather data on customer interactions and purchase histories, enabling them to deliver personalized content and recommendations. This level of customization not only enhances customer satisfaction but also increases the likelihood of conversions, as potential buyers are more inclined to engage with brands that understand their needs and preferences.

Predictive analytics plays a significant role in the marketing automation landscape, providing small business owners with insights that drive informed decision-making. By analyzing historical data and identifying patterns, predictive analytics can forecast future sales trends and customer behaviors. This functionality allows entrepreneurs to allocate resources effectively, optimize marketing strategies, and anticipate customer needs. For small businesses that may lack the manpower for extensive market research, these data-driven insights can be invaluable in crafting campaigns that resonate with their target audience.

As e-commerce continues to thrive, personalized AI recommendations have become a cornerstone of successful online retail strategies. Marketing automation platforms equipped with AI capabilities can analyze user behavior on e-commerce sites, providing tailored product suggestions that enhance the shopping experience. For small businesses operating in the digital marketplace, implementing these AI-driven recommendations can lead to increased average order values and improved customer loyalty. The ability to offer personalized shopping experiences not only differentiates a brand in a crowded market but also fosters long-term relationships with customers.

Finally, the integration of marketing automation with human resources and talent acquisition processes cannot be overlooked. Small businesses often face challenges in managing recruitment and employee engagement due to limited resources. AI solutions can streamline these processes by automating candidate sourcing, screening, and communication. By utilizing data-driven decision-making tools, entrepreneurs can ensure that they attract and retain top talent, which is essential for sustaining growth and efficiency. In this way, marketing automation transcends traditional marketing functions, becoming a vital part of a holistic approach to business development that encompasses all facets of an organization.

Key AI Tools for Marketing

In the rapidly evolving landscape of marketing, small business owners and entrepreneurs are increasingly turning to artificial intelligence tools to enhance their strategies and drive growth. These tools not only streamline processes but also enable businesses to leverage data in ways that were previously unimaginable. By integrating AI-driven marketing automation tools, small enterprises can optimize their outreach efforts, personalize customer interactions, and ultimately improve conversion rates. This chapter explores key AI tools that are transforming the marketing landscape for small businesses.

One of the most impactful AI tools for marketing is predictive analytics, which allows businesses to forecast sales and understand customer behavior with remarkable accuracy. By analyzing historical data, predictive analytics tools can identify trends and patterns that inform decision-making. Small business owners can utilize these insights to tailor their marketing strategies, allocate resources more effectively, and anticipate customer needs. This predictive capability is particularly beneficial for entrepreneurs looking to make data-driven decisions that enhance overall performance and profitability.

Personalization is another critical area where AI tools have made significant strides. E-commerce platforms can harness AI solutions to deliver personalized recommendations to customers based on their browsing and purchasing history. These personalized experiences not only improve customer engagement but also increase the likelihood of repeat purchases. Small business owners can implement AI-driven recommendation engines to create targeted marketing campaigns that resonate with specific customer segments, thereby fostering loyalty and driving sales.

In addition to marketing automation and personalization, AI solutions are also revolutionizing human resources and talent acquisition processes. Small businesses often struggle with recruiting top talent due to limited resources. AI tools can streamline recruitment by automating the screening of resumes, assessing candidates' fit for positions, and even conducting initial interviews. This not only saves time but also ensures that small businesses can attract and retain the best talent available in a competitive job market.

Finally, data-driven decision-making tools powered by AI provide entrepreneurs with the insights necessary to navigate their business environments effectively. These tools aggregate and analyze vast amounts of data, enabling business owners to make informed choices based on real-time information. For small business owners and entrepreneurs, utilizing these AI solutions is essential for identifying growth opportunities, optimizing marketing strategies, and ultimately achieving sustainable success in an increasingly digital marketplace.

Implementing AI in Your Marketing Strategy

Implementing AI in your marketing strategy is no longer a luxury reserved for large corporations; it is increasingly becoming a necessity for small businesses and entrepreneurs aiming to remain competitive. The integration of AI-driven tools not only enables more efficient operations but also fosters deeper customer engagement through personalized experiences. For small business owners, understanding how to leverage these technologies can result in significant improvements in marketing outcomes, customer retention, and ultimately, revenue growth.

One of the most impactful ways to implement AI in marketing is through automation tools. These tools streamline repetitive tasks, such as email marketing, social media management, and customer segmentation. By automating these processes, entrepreneurs can focus their efforts on strategic initiatives that drive growth. For instance, AI-driven platforms can analyze customer behavior and preferences, allowing businesses to tailor their communications and offers to individual customers. This level of personalization not only enhances customer satisfaction but also increases conversion rates, making marketing efforts more effective.

Predictive analytics is another critical component of an AI-enhanced marketing strategy. Small businesses can utilize predictive analytics to forecast sales trends, enabling them to make informed decisions regarding inventory management, pricing strategies, and marketing campaigns. By analyzing historical data, AI tools can identify patterns and predict future customer behavior, allowing entrepreneurs to allocate resources more effectively. This data-driven approach minimizes risks and maximizes profits, providing a competitive edge in the marketplace.

E-commerce platforms can greatly benefit from personalized AI recommendations. Implementing AI algorithms that analyze user behavior and preferences can lead to higher engagement and sales. For small businesses operating online, these recommendations can be the difference between a casual visitor and a loyal customer. By offering tailored product suggestions, businesses can enhance the shopping experience, reducing cart abandonment rates and increasing average order values. This personalization is critical in an era where consumers expect tailored experiences that meet their unique needs.

Finally, AI solutions in human resources and talent acquisition can streamline the recruitment process, making it more efficient and effective. For small business owners, finding the right talent is essential for growth. AI-driven recruitment tools can analyze resumes, match candidates to job descriptions, and even conduct initial screening interviews. This not only saves time but also reduces bias in hiring decisions, leading to a more diverse and capable workforce. As small businesses increasingly recognize the value of data-driven decision-making, AI will play a pivotal role in shaping their marketing strategies and overall growth trajectories.

Case Studies of Successful AI Marketing

Case studies of successful AI marketing initiatives illustrate the transformative potential of AI-driven strategies for small businesses. One notable example is a boutique e-commerce retailer that integrated AI-powered personalization tools into its online shopping experience. By analyzing customer behavior and preferences, the retailer was able to deliver tailored product recommendations, significantly enhancing the shopping experience. This approach not only increased average order value by 25% but also improved customer retention rates, demonstrating the effectiveness of personalized marketing in driving sales.

Another compelling case involves a small software development firm that embraced predictive analytics for sales forecasting. By leveraging AI algorithms to analyze historical sales data and market trends, the company gained valuable insights into customer purchasing patterns. This enabled the firm to optimize its inventory management and align its marketing efforts with anticipated demand. As a result, the company experienced a 30% increase in forecasting accuracy, allowing for more informed decision-making and resource allocation, ultimately leading to higher profitability.

In the realm of human resources, a small business specializing in recruitment adopted AI solutions to streamline its talent acquisition process. By utilizing AI-driven applicant tracking systems, the company was able to sift through resumes more efficiently, identifying the best candidates based on specific criteria. This not only reduced the time spent on hiring by 40% but also improved the quality of hires. The integration of AI in recruitment processes exemplifies how small businesses can leverage technology to enhance operational efficiency and gain a competitive edge in the job market.

A local restaurant chain also serves as an excellent case study of AI applications in marketing. The chain utilized AI-driven customer feedback analysis to understand dining preferences and customer satisfaction levels. By implementing a system that monitored online reviews and social media mentions, the restaurant was able to make data-informed changes to its menu and service offerings. This proactive approach led to a 15% increase in customer satisfaction scores, demonstrating how data-driven insights can help small businesses adapt and thrive in a competitive environment.

Finally, a small marketing agency focused on serving local clients successfully integrated AI marketing automation tools to optimize its campaign management. By automating repetitive tasks such as email marketing and social media posting, the agency could allocate more time to strategic planning and creative development. The use of AI not only improved operational efficiency but also resulted in a 50% increase in campaign effectiveness, underscoring the impact of automation on small business growth. These case studies exemplify how diverse applications of AI can drive success for small enterprises, highlighting the importance of embracing technology in today's dynamic market landscape.

Chapter 3: Predictive Analytics for Sales Forecasting

The Role of Predictive Analytics in Sales

Predictive analytics is transforming the landscape of sales for small businesses by offering a data-driven approach that enhances decision-making and optimizes revenue generation. At its core, predictive analytics utilizes historical data, statistical algorithms, and machine learning techniques to identify the likelihood of future outcomes. For small business owners and entrepreneurs, this means gaining actionable insights into customer behavior, market trends, and sales performance. By leveraging these insights, businesses can tailor their strategies to meet the evolving demands of their customers, ultimately driving sales growth and improving operational efficiency.

One of the primary applications of predictive analytics in sales is forecasting. Traditional sales forecasting methods often rely on gut feelings or outdated models, which can lead to inaccurate predictions and missed opportunities. Predictive analytics, on the other hand, employs sophisticated algorithms that analyze vast amounts of data to provide more accurate sales forecasts. This capability allows entrepreneurs to anticipate demand fluctuations, allocate resources effectively, and make informed decisions about inventory management and staffing. In a competitive marketplace, having a reliable sales forecast can be the difference between success and failure.

Moreover, predictive analytics empowers small business owners to enhance customer personalization. By analyzing customer data, predictive models can identify patterns and preferences that inform marketing strategies. Businesses can create targeted campaigns that resonate with specific segments of their audience, increasing the likelihood of conversion. For example, e-commerce platforms can utilize predictive analytics to recommend products based on previous purchases and browsing behavior, thereby improving the customer experience and driving higher sales. Personalization not only fosters customer loyalty but also differentiates a brand in a crowded market.

Integrating predictive analytics with AI-driven marketing automation tools further amplifies its effectiveness. Entrepreneurs can automate personalized outreach based on predictive insights, ensuring that the right message reaches the right customer at the right time. This level of automation not only saves time but also enhances engagement, as customers are more likely to respond to communications relevant to their interests. As small businesses increasingly adopt these technologies, they can compete more effectively with larger enterprises, leveling the playing field and enabling growth.

Finally, the role of predictive analytics extends beyond sales and marketing; it also impacts human resources and talent acquisition. By analyzing employee performance data and market trends, predictive analytics can help small business owners identify the skills and attributes needed for future hires. This data-driven approach to recruitment ensures that businesses attract and retain the right talent, which is crucial for sustaining growth. As small business owners embrace predictive analytics, they position themselves not only to thrive in their sales efforts but also to build a resilient and adaptive workforce, ultimately leading to long-term success in an ever-evolving business environment.

Tools for Predictive Sales Analytics

In the rapidly evolving landscape of small businesses, predictive sales analytics has emerged as a critical component for growth and efficiency. Entrepreneurs seeking to leverage data for improved decision-making can benefit immensely from a variety of tools designed specifically for predictive analytics. These tools enable business owners to analyze past sales data, identify trends, and forecast future sales performance, thereby facilitating informed strategic planning. By incorporating predictive analytics, small businesses can not only enhance their sales strategies but also optimize their marketing efforts and resource allocation, ultimately leading to increased profitability.

One of the most popular tools in predictive sales analytics is customer relationship management (CRM) software, which often includes built-in analytics capabilities. These platforms allow entrepreneurs to track customer interactions, manage contacts, and analyze sales data in real time. Advanced CRMs integrate AI algorithms that can predict customer behavior based on historical data, enabling businesses to tailor their marketing campaigns and sales approaches to specific customer segments. This level of personalization not only improves customer engagement but also increases the likelihood of conversion, making CRMs an indispensable tool for small business owners.

Another significant category of tools for predictive sales analytics includes data visualization software. These platforms transform complex data sets into intuitive visual formats, making it easier for entrepreneurs to identify trends and insights. With visual dashboards and reports, small business owners can quickly understand their sales performance, customer preferences, and market dynamics. Tools like Tableau and Power BI empower entrepreneurs to explore their data interactively, enabling them to make data-driven decisions that can significantly enhance their competitive edge. By presenting data visually, these tools help demystify analytics and make it accessible even for those with limited technical expertise.

Furthermore, machine learning platforms play a pivotal role in predictive analytics by allowing businesses to build models that can forecast sales trends based on various factors such as seasonality, marketing efforts, and economic indicators. Entrepreneurs can utilize platforms like Google Cloud AI and Microsoft Azure to develop custom predictive models tailored to their specific business needs. These tools not only streamline the process of building complex algorithms but also provide pre-trained models that can be fine-tuned for individual business contexts. By harnessing the power of machine learning, small businesses can gain deeper insights into their sales processes and make proactive adjustments to their strategies.

Lastly, integrating e-commerce analytics tools can significantly enhance predictive sales analytics for online businesses. These platforms analyze user behavior, shopping patterns, and conversion rates to provide actionable insights that drive sales growth. By leveraging AI-driven recommendations, entrepreneurs can personalize the shopping experience for their customers, increasing customer satisfaction and loyalty. Tools like Google Analytics and Shopify Analytics offer comprehensive data analysis capabilities, enabling small business owners to not only track performance but also predict future sales trends based on customer interactions. By utilizing these tools effectively, entrepreneurs can optimize their e-commerce strategies, ensuring sustained growth in an increasingly competitive digital marketplace.

Interpreting Data for Better Sales Forecasts

Interpreting data effectively is crucial for small business owners and entrepreneurs who seek to enhance their sales forecasts. As the market becomes increasingly competitive, leveraging data analytics provides a strategic advantage. By understanding trends, customer behaviors, and market dynamics through data interpretation, entrepreneurs can make informed decisions that drive growth. This chapter will explore how data interpretation techniques can be applied to improve sales forecasting accuracy and ultimately contribute to business success.

The first step in interpreting data for better sales forecasts is gathering relevant information from various sources. Small businesses can utilize AI-driven marketing automation tools to collect data from websites, social media platforms, and customer interactions. These tools can analyze customer behavior, preferences, and purchasing patterns, providing valuable insights that are essential for making accurate predictions. By consolidating data from diverse channels, entrepreneurs can create a comprehensive view of their market and identify key trends that may influence future sales.

Once the data is collected, the next phase involves analyzing it through predictive analytics. This technique uses historical data to forecast future sales by identifying patterns and correlations. Small business owners can employ AI solutions that automate this process, making it easier to interpret large datasets. For instance, machine learning algorithms can evaluate past sales data alongside external factors such as seasonality or economic indicators, enabling entrepreneurs to anticipate fluctuations in demand. This proactive approach allows businesses to adjust their strategies in advance, maximizing opportunities and minimizing risks.

Personalized AI recommendations play a significant role in refining sales forecasts. By utilizing customer segmentation and behavior analysis, small businesses can tailor their offerings to meet the unique needs of different customer groups. AI-driven platforms can suggest products or services based on previous purchases, enhancing customer experiences and increasing the likelihood of repeat sales.

This level of personalization not only boosts customer satisfaction but also provides entrepreneurs with more accurate data on which to base their forecasts, as they can better predict how different segments will respond to marketing efforts.

Lastly, data-driven decision-making tools empower entrepreneurs to implement their insights effectively. With the ability to visualize and interpret data through user-friendly dashboards and reports, small business owners can make strategic choices with confidence. These tools enable them to monitor performance in real-time, adjust sales strategies dynamically, and allocate resources efficiently. By fostering a culture of data-driven decision-making, entrepreneurs can enhance their sales forecasting processes, leading to sustained growth and competitive advantage in the marketplace. In an era where technology and data intertwine, mastering data interpretation is essential for any entrepreneur looking to thrive.

Real-World Applications and Success Stories

Real-world applications of artificial intelligence (AI) have transformed the landscape for small businesses and entrepreneurs, offering innovative solutions that enhance efficiency and drive growth. From AI-driven marketing automation tools to predictive analytics for sales forecasting, these technologies enable small enterprises to compete more effectively in a rapidly evolving marketplace. By examining various success stories, we can gain valuable insights into how AI can be leveraged to optimize operations, improve customer engagement, and ultimately increase profitability.

One notable success story comes from a small e-commerce business that implemented personalized AI recommendations to enhance its customer experience. By utilizing machine learning algorithms, the business was able to analyze customer behavior and preferences, delivering tailored product suggestions that significantly increased conversion rates. Over a six-month period, the company witnessed a 30% rise in sales, demonstrating the power of AI in creating personalized shopping experiences that resonate with consumers. This case exemplifies how small businesses can harness AI to drive customer loyalty and boost revenue.

In the realm of marketing automation, another small business adopted AI tools to streamline its outreach efforts. By integrating AI-driven platforms, the entrepreneur was able to automate social media postings, email marketing campaigns, and customer segmentation. This not only saved time but also enabled the business to focus on crafting more strategic marketing initiatives. As a result, the company reported a 40% increase in engagement rates and a significant reduction in marketing costs, showcasing the efficiency gains that AI can offer to small enterprises looking to maximize their marketing efforts.

Predictive analytics has also emerged as a game-changer for small businesses, particularly in sales forecasting. A small retail chain implemented predictive analytics tools to analyze historical sales data and market trends, allowing them to make informed inventory decisions. By accurately predicting demand, the business reduced excess stock by 25%, minimized lost sales due to stockouts, and improved overall cash flow. This success story highlights the importance of data-driven decision-making in ensuring that small businesses can thrive in competitive environments.

Moreover, AI solutions for human resources and talent acquisition have proved invaluable for small enterprises striving to build strong teams. A startup utilized AI-driven recruitment tools to streamline its hiring process, significantly reducing the time spent on candidate screening. By automating resume evaluations and leveraging predictive analytics to assess candidate fit, the startup was able to hire quality candidates more efficiently. This led to a 50% decrease in time-to-hire and improved employee retention rates. Such examples illustrate how AI can empower small business owners to optimize their human resources processes, enabling them to focus on strategic growth initiatives.

The integration of AI into small business operations is not just a trend; it is a necessity for those looking to enhance their competitive edge. Through real-world applications and success stories, it becomes evident that AI-driven tools can transform various aspects of business, from marketing and sales to human resources. Small business owners and entrepreneurs who embrace these technologies will not only improve their operational efficiency but also position themselves for sustained success in an increasingly digital economy.

Chapter 4: Personalized AI Recommendations for E-Commerce

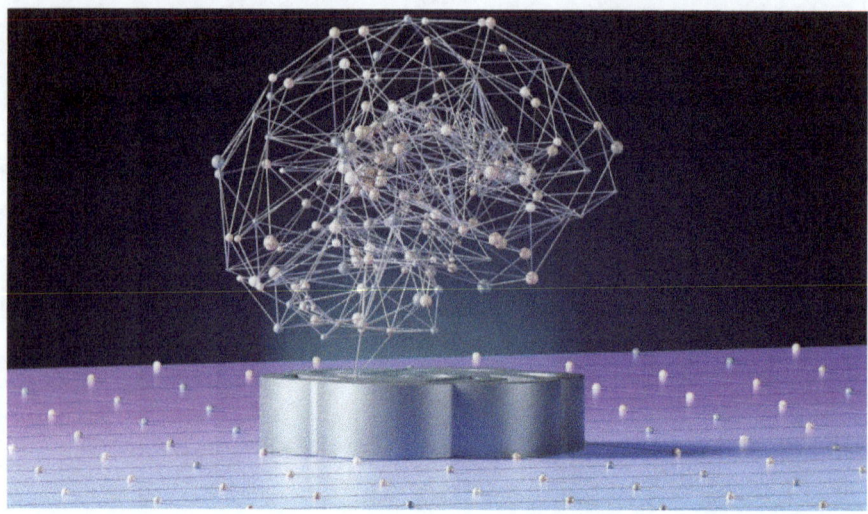

The Importance of Personalization in E-Commerce

Personalization in e-commerce has emerged as a cornerstone for success in the competitive digital marketplace. For small business owners and entrepreneurs, understanding and implementing personalized experiences can significantly enhance customer engagement and loyalty. In an era where consumers are inundated with choices, providing tailored experiences helps businesses stand out. Personalization not only boosts customer satisfaction but also increases conversion rates, making it a vital strategy for those looking to leverage AI-driven marketing automation tools.

The impact of personalization extends beyond mere customer satisfaction; it directly influences sales growth. By analyzing customer data, businesses can identify preferences and behaviors, allowing them to offer tailored recommendations that resonate with individual consumers. Predictive analytics plays a crucial role here, as it enables small enterprises to forecast trends and consumer needs more accurately. This data-driven approach empowers business owners to craft targeted marketing campaigns and optimize their product offerings, ultimately driving higher revenue.

Implementing personalized AI recommendations requires a strategic approach to data collection and analysis. Small businesses can harness various AI solutions to gather insights from customer interactions across multiple channels. By utilizing these insights, entrepreneurs can create a seamless shopping experience that anticipates customer needs, thereby fostering trust and encouraging repeat purchases. This level of customization is increasingly expected by consumers, making it essential for small businesses to adapt their strategies accordingly.

Moreover, personalization is not limited to marketing efforts; it also extends to customer service and human resources. By leveraging AI tools, businesses can provide personalized support to customers, enhancing their overall experience. Similarly, in talent acquisition, AI can help identify candidates who align with the company culture and values, streamlining the hiring process. Such personalized approaches not only improve operational efficiency but also contribute to a more cohesive brand identity.

In conclusion, the importance of personalization in e-commerce cannot be overstated. For small business owners and entrepreneurs, embracing AI-driven personalization strategies is not merely an option; it is a necessity for growth and sustainability in an increasingly digital landscape. By focusing on personalized customer experiences and leveraging data-driven insights, businesses can foster deeper connections with their audience, drive sales, and ultimately thrive in the competitive e-commerce environment.

AI Tools for Personalized Recommendations

In the rapidly evolving landscape of digital commerce, personalized recommendations powered by artificial intelligence have emerged as a cornerstone for small businesses looking to enhance customer engagement and drive sales. These AI tools leverage vast amounts of data to analyze consumer behavior, preferences, and purchasing patterns, allowing businesses to tailor their offerings to individual customers. This not only improves user experience but also increases conversion rates, ultimately contributing to a more robust bottom line. For entrepreneurs and small business owners, investing in AI-driven recommendation systems is no longer a luxury but a necessity to remain competitive in a crowded marketplace.

One of the most significant advantages of AI tools for personalized recommendations is their ability to process and analyze data at unprecedented speeds. By utilizing machine learning algorithms, businesses can gain insights into customer behaviors that were previously difficult to discern. For instance, AI can identify trends based on customers' browsing history, purchase history, and even social media interactions. This data can be harnessed to suggest products or services that align closely with individual preferences, enhancing the likelihood of repeat purchases and fostering brand loyalty. The implementation of these systems can be particularly beneficial for e-commerce platforms, where tailored suggestions can significantly influence buying decisions.

Furthermore, predictive analytics plays a crucial role in refining personalized recommendations. By forecasting future purchasing behavior based on historical data, small businesses can anticipate customer needs and preferences before they even express them. This proactive approach not only improves customer satisfaction but also allows entrepreneurs to optimize inventory management and marketing strategies. For example, if an AI tool indicates that a particular product category is likely to see increased demand, businesses can adjust their stock levels accordingly, minimizing excess inventory and maximizing sales opportunities. This level of foresight is invaluable for small enterprises striving to maintain agility in their operations.

AI solutions extend beyond e-commerce and marketing; they also hold significant promise for human resources and talent acquisition. AI-driven platforms can analyze resumes and candidate profiles to recommend the best fits for open positions based on a company's specific needs and culture. By streamlining the recruitment process, small business owners can save time and resources while ensuring they attract top talent. These tools can also be utilized to provide personalized learning and development recommendations for employees, further enhancing workforce engagement and productivity.

Ultimately, the integration of AI tools for personalized recommendations empowers small business owners to make data-driven decisions that foster growth and efficiency. By harnessing the power of artificial intelligence, entrepreneurs can not only enhance customer experiences but also streamline operations across various facets of their businesses. As the digital landscape continues to evolve, those who embrace these innovative solutions will be well-positioned to thrive in an increasingly competitive environment, ensuring long-term success and sustainability.

Enhancing User Experience through AI

Enhancing user experience through artificial intelligence (AI) is a transformative approach that small business owners can leverage to create more engaging, efficient, and personalized interactions with their customers. In a competitive marketplace, understanding the nuances of customer behavior and preferences becomes paramount. AI-driven tools provide insights that enable businesses to tailor their offerings and communications, enhancing overall satisfaction. By utilizing data analytics, entrepreneurs can decode customer journeys, ensuring that every touchpoint aligns with their needs and expectations.

AI-powered marketing automation tools exemplify how technology can streamline processes while enhancing user experience. These platforms analyze customer data to optimize marketing campaigns, delivering the right message at the right time. For small businesses, this means not only saving resources but also improving engagement rates. Automated email campaigns, personalized content recommendations, and targeted advertisements can effectively reach potential customers, fostering a relationship built on relevance and timeliness. As marketing becomes increasingly automated, the challenge lies in maintaining a human touch, which AI can support by personalizing interactions based on individual preferences.

Predictive analytics stands out as a key component in sales forecasting for small enterprises. By analyzing historical data and identifying patterns, AI tools can predict future sales trends with remarkable accuracy. This capability empowers entrepreneurs to make informed decisions regarding inventory management, staffing, and marketing strategies. Effective use of predictive analytics not only minimizes risks associated with overstocking or understocking but also enhances customer satisfaction by ensuring that popular products are readily available. Thus, entrepreneurs can stay one step ahead of market demands, ultimately improving the user experience.

E-commerce platforms can greatly benefit from personalized AI recommendations, which play a crucial role in driving sales and enhancing customer satisfaction. By analyzing user behavior, AI algorithms can suggest products that align with individual preferences, creating a tailored shopping experience. This level of personalization encourages customers to explore more, increasing the likelihood of conversion. Additionally, implementing AI-driven chatbots can provide immediate support and assistance, addressing customer queries in real time. This seamless integration of AI not only enhances the shopping experience but also builds customer loyalty by making users feel valued and understood.

Lastly, AI solutions for human resources and talent acquisition contribute to a more efficient and user-friendly hiring process. By utilizing AI-powered tools, small businesses can streamline recruitment workflows, ensuring that candidates are matched with roles that suit their skills and experiences. This not only improves the candidate experience but also enhances the quality of hires, ultimately benefiting the organization. Moreover, data-driven decision-making tools enable entrepreneurs to analyze employee performance and satisfaction, fostering a positive workplace culture.

By prioritizing user experience within their teams, entrepreneurs can cultivate an environment that attracts and retains top talent, further driving their business success.

Measuring the Impact of Personalization

Measuring the impact of personalization is crucial for small business owners and entrepreneurs looking to leverage artificial intelligence effectively. Personalization refers to tailoring products, services, and experiences to individual customers based on their preferences and behaviors. In an era where consumers expect tailored interactions, understanding how personalization affects customer engagement, retention, and sales becomes essential. By utilizing data-driven analytics, small businesses can assess the efficacy of their personalization strategies and make informed decisions to enhance their offerings.

One of the primary metrics to consider when measuring the impact of personalization is customer engagement. This can be quantified through various indicators, such as click-through rates, time spent on site, and interactions with personalized content. By implementing AI-driven marketing automation tools, businesses can analyze how personalized recommendations influence user behavior. For instance, tracking how personalized email campaigns lead to increased open and conversion rates can provide valuable insights into consumer preferences and the effectiveness of tailored content.

Customer retention is another vital aspect of personalization that should be measured. A personalized experience can significantly increase customer loyalty, leading to repeat purchases and long-term relationships. Metrics such as the customer lifetime value (CLV) and churn rate can help entrepreneurs evaluate the success of their personalization efforts. Predictive analytics can also play a role in anticipating customer needs, allowing businesses to adjust their strategies proactively and improve customer satisfaction over time.

Sales performance serves as a direct indicator of the success of personalized marketing initiatives. By utilizing AI solutions for e-commerce platforms, small businesses can track sales data before and after implementing personalization strategies. This includes monitoring average order values, conversion rates, and overall revenue growth. Analyzing these metrics enables entrepreneurs to determine which personalized strategies yield the highest return on investment and to refine their approach based on empirical evidence.

Finally, integrating feedback loops into the measurement process is essential for continuous improvement. Utilizing data-driven decision-making tools, entrepreneurs can gather insights from customer interactions and preferences. This feedback can inform future personalization efforts, ensuring that businesses remain agile and responsive to market demands. By routinely measuring the impact of personalization through these various metrics, small business owners can cultivate a culture of data-informed growth, ultimately leading to enhanced customer experiences and increased profitability.

Chapter 5: AI Solutions for Human Resources and Talent Acquisition

The Evolving Role of AI in HR

The integration of artificial intelligence into human resources (HR) represents a significant evolution in the way small businesses approach talent acquisition and management. Traditionally, HR functions relied heavily on manual processes and subjective assessments, which often led to inefficiencies and biases. With the advent of AI-driven solutions, small business owners can streamline their recruitment processes, reduce time-to-hire, and improve the quality of their hires. By leveraging AI tools for resume screening, candidate matching, and even initial interview scheduling, entrepreneurs can focus on strategic decision-making while allowing technology to handle time-consuming administrative tasks.

AI is also transforming how organizations engage with their employees post-hire. Employee experience has become a critical factor in retaining talent, and AI-driven analytics provide insights into employee sentiment and engagement levels. For small businesses, understanding these dynamics can lead to more tailored employee development programs and improved workplace cultures. Tools that analyze employee feedback and performance data enable entrepreneurs to make data-driven decisions to enhance morale and productivity, ensuring that their teams remain motivated and aligned with business objectives.

Moreover, predictive analytics has emerged as a powerful tool for small businesses in forecasting workforce needs and optimizing talent acquisition strategies. By analyzing historical hiring data and market trends, AI can help entrepreneurs anticipate future staffing requirements, allowing them to proactively seek out talent before critical gaps emerge. This forward-thinking approach not only enhances operational efficiency but also positions small businesses to respond swiftly to changes in the market landscape, thereby maintaining a competitive edge.

Personalized AI recommendations are also making waves in the realm of HR. For instance, these tools can suggest tailored training and development programs based on individual employee performance and career aspirations. This level of personalization not only fosters a culture of continuous learning but also empowers employees to take charge of their professional growth. Small business owners who implement these AI solutions can create a more engaged workforce that is aligned with the company's goals and values, ultimately driving better business outcomes.

As the role of AI in HR continues to evolve, small business owners must remain open to adopting these technologies to stay ahead in a rapidly changing environment. Embracing AI-driven tools not only enhances operational efficiency but also contributes to a more dynamic and responsive workplace. By investing in AI solutions for HR and talent acquisition, entrepreneurs can build stronger teams, foster innovation, and drive sustainable growth, establishing a solid foundation for their businesses in the years to come.

Tools for Recruitment and Talent Management

In the evolving landscape of entrepreneurship, small business owners are increasingly leveraging technology to streamline their recruitment and talent management processes. The integration of artificial intelligence into these domains not only enhances efficiency but also allows for more strategic decision-making. AI-driven recruitment tools can sift through mountains of resumes, identifying the most suitable candidates based on predefined criteria. This automation reduces the time spent on initial candidate screening, allowing business owners to focus on more critical aspects of their operations while ensuring that they attract top talent.

Moreover, talent management has become more data-centric with the advent of predictive analytics. These tools enable small enterprises to forecast employee performance and retention rates based on historical data. By analyzing patterns and trends in employee behavior, businesses can implement targeted strategies to enhance workforce engagement and productivity. This proactive approach allows entrepreneurs to address potential issues before they escalate, ultimately fostering a more resilient and motivated team.

In addition to recruitment and retention, personalized AI recommendations are transforming the way small businesses approach training and development. AI solutions can assess the skills of employees and recommend tailored training programs that align with both individual capabilities and organizational goals. This customization not only accelerates skill acquisition but also boosts employee satisfaction, as team members feel supported in their professional growth. Consequently, this targeted development approach contributes to a more competent workforce, positioning small businesses for long-term success.

Furthermore, AI-driven platforms facilitate improved communication and collaboration within teams. Tools that incorporate natural language processing and machine learning can analyze team interactions, providing insights into collaboration patterns and identifying areas for improvement. This data-driven approach fosters a culture of transparency and open communication, essential elements for any successful business environment. By harnessing these tools, entrepreneurs can create a more cohesive and effective team dynamic, ultimately driving business performance.

Finally, the importance of data-driven decision-making in recruitment and talent management cannot be overstated. Small business owners equipped with AI analytics tools can make informed choices based on concrete data rather than intuition alone. This shift towards a more analytical mindset helps in optimizing recruitment strategies, enhancing employee satisfaction, and driving overall organizational performance. As the landscape continues to evolve, embracing these AI solutions will be crucial for small enterprises seeking to maintain a competitive edge in the marketplace.

Enhancing Employee Engagement through AI
Enhancing employee engagement is vital for fostering a productive

and motivated workforce, especially in small businesses where every team member's input can significantly impact overall performance. AI technologies offer innovative solutions to enhance engagement by streamlining communication, personalizing experiences, and automating repetitive tasks. By integrating AI-driven tools, small business owners can create a more dynamic and inclusive workplace that not only attracts top talent but also retains them through meaningful engagement strategies.

One of the primary ways AI enhances employee engagement is through improved communication channels. AI-powered chatbots and virtual assistants can facilitate real-time interactions, ensuring that employees have access to the information they need when they need it. These tools can handle routine inquiries about company policies, project updates, or HR-related questions, freeing up valuable time for managers to focus on strategic initiatives. As a result, employees feel more supported and engaged, knowing their concerns are addressed promptly, which fosters a culture of transparency and openness.

In addition to enhancing communication, AI can personalize the employee experience by offering tailored recommendations for professional development and training. Machine learning algorithms can analyze individual performance data and career aspirations, suggesting relevant courses or mentorship programs that align with each employee's goals. This personalized approach not only empowers employees to take charge of their own development but also signals to them that the organization values their growth. When employees see that their company is invested in their success, their engagement levels are likely to increase.

Moreover, AI-driven analytics can provide valuable insights into employee engagement metrics. By leveraging predictive analytics, small business owners can identify trends and patterns related to employee satisfaction, turnover rates, and productivity levels. This data-driven approach allows leaders to make informed decisions about engagement strategies, ensuring they are addressing the specific needs and concerns of their workforce. With real-time feedback mechanisms, businesses can adapt their strategies promptly, creating an agile work environment that continuously evolves to meet the demands of both employees and the market.

Finally, integrating AI solutions into human resources and talent acquisition processes can significantly enhance employee engagement from the outset. By utilizing AI for sourcing candidates, small businesses can identify individuals whose values and skills align with the company culture. This alignment fosters a sense of belonging and purpose among employees, enhancing engagement as they see their roles contributing to the organization's mission. Furthermore, AI can streamline onboarding processes, ensuring new hires feel welcomed and well-prepared from day one, ultimately leading to higher retention rates and a more cohesive team dynamic.

Future Trends in AI and HR

The future of artificial intelligence (AI) in human resources (HR) is poised to transform how small businesses approach talent acquisition, employee management, and organizational development. As AI technologies continue to evolve, they offer innovative solutions to streamline HR processes, making them more efficient and effective. Small business owners can leverage these advancements to enhance their recruitment strategies, improve employee experiences, and drive overall organizational performance.

One significant trend in AI and HR is the increasing use of predictive analytics for talent acquisition. Small enterprises can utilize these tools to analyze vast amounts of data, enabling them to identify the best candidates for specific roles. By predicting candidate success based on historical data and behavioral patterns, businesses can make informed hiring decisions that align with their organizational goals. This data-driven approach not only reduces the time and resources spent on recruitment but also minimizes turnover rates by ensuring a better fit between employees and the company culture.

Moreover, personalized AI recommendations are becoming essential for enhancing employee engagement and retention. Small businesses can implement AI-driven platforms that provide tailored learning and development opportunities based on individual employee needs and career aspirations. By fostering a culture of continuous learning, organizations can boost employee satisfaction and productivity. These personalized experiences can also extend to performance management, where AI tools help in setting goals, providing feedback, and recognizing achievements in real-time, thereby fostering a more engaged workforce.

Automation in HR processes is another trend that can significantly benefit small businesses. Routine tasks such as payroll processing, benefits administration, and employee onboarding can be automated through AI solutions, allowing HR professionals to focus on strategic initiatives that add value to the organization. This shift not only increases efficiency but also reduces the likelihood of errors associated with manual processes, ultimately contributing to a more streamlined HR function. With limited resources, small businesses can achieve greater operational effectiveness by adopting these AI-driven automation tools.

Lastly, the integration of AI in data-driven decision-making is transforming how small businesses approach HR challenges. By harnessing AI analytics, entrepreneurs can gain insights into workforce trends, employee performance, and overall organizational health. These insights enable business leaders to make proactive decisions that optimize talent management and align workforce capabilities with business objectives. As AI technologies continue to advance, the ability to leverage data for strategic HR decisions will become increasingly vital for small enterprises seeking to compete in a rapidly changing marketplace.

Chapter 6: Data-Driven Decision-Making Tools

Importance of Data-Driven Decisions

Data-driven decision-making has emerged as a cornerstone for success in the modern business landscape, particularly for small enterprises and entrepreneurs. In an era where data is abundant yet underutilized, the ability to harness this resource effectively can mean the difference between stagnation and growth. Small business owners who embrace data-driven strategies are better positioned to identify trends, understand customer preferences, and optimize operations. This approach not only enhances efficiency but also fosters agility in responding to market changes, allowing entrepreneurs to stay ahead of the competition.

For tech-curious individuals, understanding the significance of data in decision-making processes is vital. AI-driven tools can analyze vast amounts of information quickly, providing insights that would be impossible to obtain manually. By leveraging predictive analytics, small businesses can forecast sales trends with greater accuracy, thereby making informed inventory decisions and minimizing waste. This predictive capability is particularly beneficial for new entrepreneurs who may lack extensive market experience, as it allows them to make strategic choices grounded in empirical evidence.

In the realm of marketing automation, data-driven decision-making is equally transformative. Personalized AI recommendations not only enhance the customer experience but also drive conversion rates. By analyzing customer behavior and preferences, entrepreneurs can tailor their marketing efforts, ensuring that messages resonate with specific target audiences. This level of personalization not only boosts customer satisfaction but also increases brand loyalty, which is essential for small businesses striving to build a solid customer base in a competitive environment.

Furthermore, data-driven insights extend beyond marketing and sales; they play a crucial role in human resources and talent acquisition. Small business owners can utilize AI solutions to analyze applicant data, ensuring they select candidates who align with their organizational culture and values. This data-centric approach reduces hiring biases and enhances the quality of new hires, which is critical for the long-term success of any enterprise. By streamlining these processes, entrepreneurs can focus more on developing their businesses rather than getting bogged down in administrative tasks.

Ultimately, the importance of data-driven decisions cannot be overstated. As small businesses navigate the complexities of the digital age, those who utilize AI-driven tools to inform their strategies will be at a distinct advantage. By embracing data analytics in all facets of their operations—from marketing to hiring—entrepreneurs can cultivate a more responsive, efficient, and successful business model. The integration of data into decision-making processes not only empowers small business owners but also sets the stage for sustainable growth in an increasingly competitive landscape.

AI Tools for Data Analysis and Visualization

AI tools for data analysis and visualization are transforming how small businesses operate, enabling entrepreneurs to harness the power of their data effectively. These tools allow business owners to analyze complex datasets, uncover trends, and visualize information in ways that were previously accessible only to larger organizations with dedicated data science teams. By leveraging these advanced technologies, small business owners can make informed decisions, optimize operations, and enhance customer engagement, ultimately driving growth and efficiency.

One of the significant advantages of AI-driven data analysis tools is their ability to process vast amounts of data swiftly, providing insights that can be acted upon in real-time. For instance, platforms like Tableau and Power BI utilize machine learning algorithms to identify patterns and generate predictive models, enabling entrepreneurs to anticipate market trends and customer behaviors. These insights are crucial for effective sales forecasting, allowing small businesses to adjust their strategies proactively rather than reactively. As a result, entrepreneurs can allocate resources more efficiently, ensuring that they are not only meeting current demands but also preparing for future opportunities.

In addition to predictive analytics, AI tools also offer personalized recommendations that can significantly enhance e-commerce platforms. By analyzing customer data, these tools can suggest products tailored to individual preferences, thereby improving the shopping experience and increasing conversion rates. For small business owners, implementing AI-driven recommendation systems can lead to higher customer satisfaction and loyalty, as shoppers feel understood and valued. This personalization not only drives sales but also fosters a deeper connection between the brand and its customers, which is vital in a competitive market.

Moreover, AI solutions extend beyond customer-facing applications to human resources and talent acquisition. Tools such as Pymetrics and HireVue utilize AI to analyze resumes and assess candidates' fit based on data-driven insights. This streamlining of the hiring process is particularly beneficial for small businesses that may lack the resources to conduct extensive recruitment campaigns. By leveraging these AI tools, entrepreneurs can save time, reduce bias in hiring, and ultimately build more effective teams that align with their business goals.

Finally, the integration of AI tools for data-driven decision-making empowers small business owners to cultivate a culture of analytics within their organizations. By utilizing insights generated from AI analysis, entrepreneurs can make strategic decisions backed by solid data, rather than relying solely on intuition or anecdotal evidence. This approach not only enhances operational efficiency but also fosters innovation, as businesses become more adept at testing new ideas and quickly adapting to changes in their market landscape. As the importance of data continues to grow, embracing AI tools for data analysis and visualization will be essential for small businesses aiming to thrive in the digital age.

Best Practices for Implementing Data-Driven Strategies

Implementing data-driven strategies is crucial for small business owners and entrepreneurs aiming to harness the power of artificial intelligence. To effectively integrate these strategies, it is essential to cultivate a data-centric culture within the organization. This begins with training employees at all levels to understand the importance of data in decision-making processes. Encouraging a mindset that values data will facilitate smoother adoption of AI tools and analytics platforms. Moreover, fostering collaboration among departments can enhance the sharing of insights derived from data, leading to more informed decisions across the board.

Selecting the right tools is equally important in the implementation of data-driven strategies. Small businesses should prioritize AI-driven solutions that align with their specific needs and objectives.

For instance, e-commerce platforms can benefit from personalized AI recommendations that enhance customer engagement and drive sales. Similarly, entrepreneurs can leverage predictive analytics for sales forecasting, ensuring they make informed inventory and marketing decisions. Conducting thorough research and trials of various tools will help identify the best fit for the organization's goals.

Data quality cannot be overlooked when implementing data-driven strategies. Ensuring the accuracy, consistency, and relevance of data is paramount for deriving actionable insights. Small business owners should establish robust data governance practices, including regular audits and cleansing of data sets. Investing in training for staff on data management practices will also support the integrity of the data being used. By maintaining high data quality, businesses can make more reliable predictions and informed strategic decisions.

Furthermore, integrating feedback loops into the data strategy is a best practice that can significantly enhance the effectiveness of AI-driven initiatives. Continuous monitoring of outcomes allows businesses to adjust their strategies in real-time based on performance metrics. Utilizing analytics tools to track key performance indicators (KPIs) will help entrepreneurs identify trends and areas for improvement. This iterative approach not only optimizes existing strategies but also fosters innovation as businesses adapt to changing market conditions and customer preferences.

Lastly, small business owners should focus on establishing clear objectives for their data-driven strategies. Setting measurable goals will provide a framework for evaluating success and progress. Whether it's improving customer retention rates through targeted marketing campaigns or increasing efficiency in human resources processes with AI solutions, having defined objectives ensures that efforts are aligned with broader business goals. By adhering to these best practices, entrepreneurs can effectively implement data-driven strategies that leverage the power of AI, ultimately driving growth and operational efficiency.

Success Stories of Data-Driven Entrepreneurs

In the rapidly evolving landscape of entrepreneurship, data-driven decision-making has emerged as a cornerstone of success for small business owners. Numerous entrepreneurs have harnessed the power of data analytics and artificial intelligence to not only streamline their operations but also create innovative solutions that resonate with their target markets. These success stories serve as examples of how strategic use of data can lead to growth, efficiency, and a competitive edge, inspiring others in the tech-curious millennial demographic to embrace similar strategies.

One standout example is a small e-commerce company that leveraged personalized AI recommendations to enhance customer engagement and drive sales. By analyzing customer behavior, purchase history, and browsing patterns, the business implemented an AI-driven recommendation engine that suggested products tailored to individual preferences. The result was a significant increase in conversion rates and customer satisfaction, demonstrating how data can inform marketing strategies and improve the overall shopping experience. This case illustrates the potential of AI in creating personalized interactions that foster loyalty among consumers.

Another notable success story involves a small enterprise utilizing predictive analytics for sales forecasting. By employing sophisticated algorithms to analyze historical sales data, market trends, and external factors, the business was able to make informed predictions about future sales performance. This capability allowed the entrepreneur to optimize inventory management and fine-tune marketing campaigns, ultimately leading to improved cash flow and profitability. The power of predictive analytics showcases how small businesses can make data-driven decisions that directly impact their bottom line.

In the realm of human resources, a small startup has effectively integrated AI solutions for talent acquisition. By utilizing AI-driven platforms to sift through applications and identify the most qualified candidates based on data points such as skills, experience, and cultural fit, the business significantly reduced the time and resources spent on recruitment. This approach not only streamlined the hiring process but also improved the quality of hires, showcasing the benefits of data-driven strategies in enhancing organizational efficiency.

These success stories illustrate that the integration of AI and data analytics into business operations is not just for large corporations but is equally accessible to small entrepreneurs. By embracing data-driven tools, business owners can innovate their marketing strategies, improve customer experiences, forecast sales more accurately, and enhance their hiring processes. As these entrepreneurs demonstrate, the journey toward becoming data-driven is a vital step in navigating the complexities of the modern business landscape, ultimately leading to sustainable growth and success.

Fostering Innovation and Adaptability

Chapter 7: Building an AI-Ready Business Culture

Fostering innovation and adaptability is crucial for small business owners and entrepreneurs navigating the rapidly evolving landscape of artificial intelligence. As technology continues to advance at an unprecedented pace, businesses must not only embrace these changes but also leverage them to enhance their operations and drive growth. In this context, fostering a culture of innovation becomes essential, enabling businesses to stay ahead of the curve and effectively respond to shifting market dynamics. Embracing AI-driven tools and solutions allows business leaders to streamline processes, improve efficiency, and ultimately deliver better value to their customers.

One of the most significant advantages of AI for small businesses lies in its ability to automate routine tasks. Automation frees up valuable time and resources, enabling entrepreneurs to focus on strategic initiatives that require human creativity and judgment. For instance, AI-driven marketing automation tools can handle repetitive tasks such as email marketing, social media posting, and lead scoring. By adopting these technologies, small business owners can enhance their marketing efforts without the overhead of hiring additional staff, thus optimizing their return on investment.

Predictive analytics represents another powerful avenue for fostering innovation. By harnessing AI to analyze historical data, small businesses can forecast sales trends and customer behavior, enabling more informed decision-making. This data-driven approach allows entrepreneurs to anticipate market demands, adjust their inventory accordingly, and create targeted marketing campaigns that resonate with their audience. The ability to leverage predictive analytics not only enhances operational efficiency but also empowers entrepreneurs to make strategic decisions grounded in empirical evidence rather than gut feeling.

Personalized AI recommendations are transforming the e-commerce landscape, allowing small businesses to deliver tailored experiences to their customers. By utilizing AI algorithms that analyze customer preferences and purchasing behaviors, businesses can offer personalized product suggestions, improving customer satisfaction and boosting sales. This level of personalization helps build customer loyalty and enhances the overall shopping experience, making it imperative for small business owners to invest in AI solutions that can provide these capabilities.

Lastly, AI solutions for human resources and talent acquisition are vital for fostering a culture of adaptability within small enterprises. By implementing AI-driven tools for recruitment and employee engagement, businesses can streamline their hiring processes, identify top talent, and improve employee retention. Furthermore, data-driven decision-making tools enable entrepreneurs to assess workforce performance and identify areas for improvement. In a competitive landscape, the ability to attract and retain skilled employees is fundamental to driving innovation and ensuring long-term success. Thus, fostering a culture that embraces AI not only enhances operational capabilities but also positions small businesses for sustainable growth in the digital age.

Training Employees for AI Integration

Training employees for AI integration is a critical step for small business owners and entrepreneurs looking to leverage artificial intelligence to enhance their operations. As AI technologies become increasingly accessible, it is essential for teams to be adequately prepared to utilize these tools effectively. This involves not only understanding how AI works but also developing the skills necessary to implement AI solutions in their respective roles. A well-structured training program can empower employees to embrace AI, driving innovation and efficiency within the organization.

The first aspect of training employees is to create a foundational understanding of AI concepts and their applications. This can be achieved through workshops, online courses, or internal training sessions that cover the basics of AI, machine learning, and data analytics. Employees should learn about the types of AI tools available, such as predictive analytics for sales forecasting and AI-driven marketing automation tools. By establishing a strong knowledge base, employees will feel more comfortable engaging with AI technologies and can better identify opportunities for integration within their work processes.

In addition to foundational knowledge, hands-on training with specific AI tools is crucial. Each department may require different AI solutions, such as personalized recommendations for e-commerce platforms or AI solutions for human resources and talent acquisition. Practical training sessions should focus on how to use these tools effectively, allowing employees to experiment and learn through trial and error. By providing access to real-world scenarios, businesses can ensure that their teams not only understand the technology but also develop the confidence to utilize it in their daily tasks.

Moreover, fostering a culture of continuous learning is vital for the long-term success of AI integration. As AI technology evolves rapidly, ongoing training and development will keep employees updated on the latest advancements and best practices. Regular workshops, knowledge-sharing sessions, and access to online resources can encourage staff to stay informed and engaged. This commitment to ongoing education not only enhances employee skills but also cultivates an innovative mindset that is essential for leveraging AI's full potential.

Finally, encouraging collaboration and knowledge sharing among employees can significantly enhance the effectiveness of AI integration. By fostering an environment where team members can share insights, experiences, and challenges related to AI tools, businesses can create a supportive network that promotes collective learning. This collaborative approach not only helps in overcoming obstacles but also stimulates creativity, leading to new ideas and solutions. By investing in training and nurturing a culture of collaboration, small businesses can position themselves for success in an increasingly AI-driven marketplace.

Overcoming Resistance to Change

Resistance to change is a common challenge faced by small business owners and entrepreneurs, particularly when integrating new technologies like artificial intelligence. The apprehension often stems from a fear of the unknown, potential disruptions to established workflows, and concerns over the costs associated with implementing new systems. To effectively overcome this resistance, it is essential to foster a culture that embraces change and innovation. This involves not only communicating the benefits of AI-driven tools but also actively involving team members in the transition process, allowing them to express their concerns and contribute to solutions.

Education plays a pivotal role in alleviating fears surrounding AI and automation. Small business owners should invest time in training their teams on how AI technologies work and the advantages they can bring to everyday operations. This could include workshops, online courses, or inviting industry experts to share insights. By demystifying AI and showcasing successful case studies from similar businesses, entrepreneurs can help their teams visualize the potential impact of these tools on productivity and profitability. Understanding the technology can transform apprehension into enthusiasm, allowing employees to see themselves as integral to the change rather than as passive recipients.

In addition to education, clear communication is critical in overcoming resistance. Business leaders must articulate a compelling vision that aligns the implementation of AI tools with the overall goals of the organization. This vision should outline not only the expected outcomes but also the steps involved in the transition process. Regular updates and open dialogue can help mitigate fears and foster an environment of trust. When team members feel informed and involved, they are more likely to embrace change rather than resist it.

Furthermore, small business owners should consider implementing AI solutions incrementally. A phased approach allows teams to acclimate to new technologies gradually, minimizing disruption while providing opportunities for feedback and adjustment. For instance, starting with predictive analytics for sales forecasting can help businesses understand their customer behavior better before moving on to more complex applications like personalized AI recommendations. This step-by-step strategy not only eases the transition but also allows for the celebration of small wins that can motivate teams to continue embracing innovation.

Lastly, it is vital to recognize and address the emotional aspects of change. Resistance is often rooted in fear of job loss or the belief that new technologies will render certain skills obsolete. Entrepreneurs should reassure their teams that AI is intended to complement human capabilities, not replace them. By emphasizing the role of AI in enhancing efficiency and freeing up time for creative and strategic tasks, business leaders can help shift the narrative from one of fear to one of opportunity. Creating a supportive environment that values human input alongside technological advancements will facilitate a smoother transition and ultimately lead to a more resilient and agile organization.

Creating a Sustainable AI Strategy

Creating a sustainable AI strategy requires a comprehensive approach that aligns technological capabilities with business objectives. For small business owners and entrepreneurs, establishing a clear vision for AI integration is essential. This vision should not only focus on immediate gains but also consider long-term implications and adaptability to evolving market conditions. By articulating a robust strategy, business leaders can ensure that their AI initiatives contribute to sustainable growth, enhance operational efficiency, and drive customer satisfaction.

A critical first step in developing a sustainable AI strategy is assessing current capabilities and identifying areas where AI can add the most value. Entrepreneurs should conduct a thorough analysis of their existing processes, customer interactions, and data management practices. This assessment will help pinpoint specific pain points that AI solutions can address, such as automating repetitive tasks, improving customer engagement through personalized recommendations, or leveraging predictive analytics for sales forecasting. Understanding these needs allows businesses to prioritize AI initiatives that will yield the highest return on investment.

Once the needs are identified, it is vital to select the right AI tools and technologies that align with the business's goals. Entrepreneurs should consider solutions that are user-friendly and scalable, particularly those designed for small businesses. Automation tools for marketing, such as AI-driven email campaigns or social media management platforms, can streamline operations and enhance outreach efforts. Similarly, predictive analytics tools can empower small businesses to make informed decisions based on data trends, optimizing inventory management and sales strategies. Choosing the right tools fosters a culture of innovation and positions the business for long-term success.

Another crucial aspect of creating a sustainable AI strategy is fostering a data-driven culture within the organization. Entrepreneurs need to emphasize the importance of data collection and analysis among their teams. Training employees to interpret AI-generated insights and integrate them into decision-making processes enhances overall business agility. Additionally, leveraging AI for talent acquisition and human resources can streamline hiring processes, thereby ensuring that the right talent is brought on board to support the business's growth objectives. By prioritizing a data-centric approach, businesses can effectively harness AI technologies to drive strategic outcomes.

Lastly, continuous evaluation and adaptation of the AI strategy are imperative for sustainability. The landscape of AI is constantly evolving, with new developments and tools emerging regularly. Small business owners should establish metrics to assess the effectiveness of their AI initiatives and remain receptive to change. Regularly reviewing performance data and soliciting feedback from employees and customers can provide valuable insights into areas that require adjustment. By committing to ongoing learning and adaptation, entrepreneurs can ensure that their AI strategy remains relevant and effective in achieving long-term business objectives.

Chapter 8: Ethical Considerations and Challenges in AI

Understanding AI Ethics

Understanding AI ethics is crucial for small business owners and entrepreneurs as they navigate the rapidly evolving landscape of artificial intelligence. The implementation of AI technologies presents numerous opportunities for growth and efficiency, yet it also raises important ethical concerns. Entrepreneurs must comprehend the principles of AI ethics to ensure that their use of these technologies aligns with societal values and legal standards. This understanding fosters trust among customers and stakeholders, ultimately enhancing brand reputation and promoting responsible business practices.

One of the primary ethical considerations in AI is transparency. Small businesses leveraging AI-driven marketing automation tools or predictive analytics for sales forecasting must be clear about how these systems function and the data they utilize. Customers should be informed about how their data is collected, processed, and applied to tailor recommendations or marketing strategies. This transparency not only helps in building consumer trust but also mitigates risks associated with data misuse and privacy violations.

Another significant aspect of AI ethics is fairness. Entrepreneurs must be vigilant about ensuring that their AI solutions do not perpetuate biases. For instance, when utilizing AI for human resources and talent acquisition, it is essential to ensure that algorithms do not favor certain demographics over others. Training datasets must be representative and diverse to avoid reinforcing existing inequalities. By prioritizing fairness in AI applications, small businesses can create a more inclusive environment and attract a broader customer base.

Accountability is also a key principle in the ethical deployment of AI technologies. Small business owners should establish clear guidelines and frameworks for accountability, especially when using data-driven decision-making tools. This involves understanding who is responsible for the outcomes generated by AI systems and being prepared to address any negative impacts that may arise. By implementing robust accountability measures, entrepreneurs can safeguard their operations against potential legal and reputational risks.

Finally, fostering a culture of ethical AI use within an organization is essential for sustainable growth. Business leaders should educate their teams about AI ethics and encourage discussions around ethical dilemmas that may arise in the course of using AI technologies. This culture not only promotes responsible use of AI but also empowers employees to identify and mitigate ethical risks proactively. By embracing ethical principles in their AI strategies, small business owners can position themselves as leaders in responsible AI innovation, ultimately driving long-term success in the marketplace.

Addressing Bias and Fairness in AI Tools

Addressing bias and fairness in AI tools is an essential consideration for small business owners and entrepreneurs who wish to leverage artificial intelligence effectively. As organizations increasingly adopt AI-driven solutions, it is crucial to understand that these technologies can inadvertently perpetuate existing biases present in the data they are trained on. This can lead to unfair treatment of customers or employees, damaging reputations and ultimately affecting business performance. Entrepreneurs must recognize that while AI can enhance efficiency and decision-making, the integrity of these tools relies heavily on the quality and diversity of the data used.

To combat bias, small business owners should prioritize selecting AI tools that have undergone rigorous fairness assessments. This involves scrutinizing the algorithms and datasets employed by these tools to ensure they do not favor certain demographics over others. Engaging with vendors who are transparent about their methodologies and who actively work to eliminate bias can significantly enhance the reliability of AI applications in marketing automation, sales forecasting, and human resources. It is essential to ask questions about the training data and the steps taken to ensure fairness, thereby fostering a more equitable environment in which all stakeholders can thrive.

Moreover, entrepreneurs should consider implementing regular audits of their AI tools to identify and rectify any biases that may arise over time. This proactive approach allows businesses to remain vigilant against evolving biases that could influence customer interactions and internal processes. By continuously monitoring AI outputs and their impact, small business owners can make informed adjustments that promote fairness and accountability. Such practices not only reinforce ethical standards but also build trust among customers and employees, who increasingly expect businesses to act responsibly in their use of technology.

Another critical aspect of addressing bias in AI is the involvement of diverse teams in the development and deployment of these tools. Diverse perspectives can help identify potential pitfalls in AI applications, ensuring that the tools serve a broader audience without marginalizing specific groups. For entrepreneurs focused on personalized AI recommendations or data-driven decision-making, fostering inclusivity in the development process can lead to more comprehensive solutions that meet the varied needs of their customer base. This collaborative approach enhances creativity and innovation, ultimately driving better business outcomes.

Finally, education plays a pivotal role in addressing bias and fairness in AI. Entrepreneurs and their teams should invest in training and resources that enhance their understanding of AI ethics and bias mitigation strategies. This knowledge empowers small business owners to make informed decisions when selecting and implementing AI tools, ensuring that their organizations remain competitive while upholding ethical standards. As AI continues to evolve, a commitment to fairness will not only enhance business efficiency but also contribute to a more just and equitable marketplace, positioning small businesses as leaders in responsible AI adoption.

Compliance and Legal Considerations

Compliance and legal considerations are paramount in the rapidly evolving landscape of artificial intelligence. As small business owners and entrepreneurs leverage AI-driven technologies to optimize operations and enhance customer experiences, it is crucial to navigate the complex regulatory environment governing data usage, privacy, and ethical standards. Familiarity with relevant laws, such as the General Data Protection Regulation (GDPR) and the California Consumer Privacy Act (CCPA), is essential for ensuring compliance and avoiding potential legal pitfalls. These regulations mandate transparency in data collection and processing, highlighting the importance of obtaining informed consent from users.

Moreover, understanding intellectual property rights related to AI-generated outputs is vital for safeguarding innovations. Entrepreneurs need to consider how their AI solutions may interact with existing patents and copyrights, particularly in the context of content generation and software development. Establishing clear ownership of AI-generated works not only protects the business's intellectual property but also mitigates the risk of infringement claims from competitors. Small business owners should consult legal experts to navigate these complexities and develop robust agreements that delineate rights and responsibilities regarding AI technologies.

Data security is another critical aspect of compliance that entrepreneurs must prioritize. The use of AI often involves the collection and analysis of vast amounts of sensitive data, which can make businesses vulnerable to cyber threats. Implementing strong data protection measures, such as encryption and regular security audits, is essential to safeguard customer information and comply with applicable data protection laws. Additionally, businesses should establish clear protocols for data breach response and notification to ensure compliance with legal requirements and maintain customer trust.

As AI technologies continue to advance, ethical considerations surrounding their use are increasingly coming to the forefront. Entrepreneurs must be vigilant about the implications of AI-driven decision-making, particularly in areas such as hiring, marketing, and customer interactions. Bias in AI algorithms can lead to discriminatory outcomes, so it is imperative to adopt practices that promote fairness and accountability. Regularly auditing AI systems for biases and ensuring diverse data sets can help mitigate these risks, allowing businesses to leverage AI responsibly while adhering to ethical standards.

Finally, ongoing education and training in compliance and legal matters are essential for entrepreneurs aiming to harness the full potential of AI. Engaging with legal professionals, attending workshops, and participating in industry forums can provide valuable insights into the latest developments in AI regulations and best practices. By fostering a culture of compliance and ethical awareness within their organizations, small business owners can not only protect themselves from legal repercussions but also enhance their brand reputation in an increasingly conscientious marketplace. This proactive approach will enable them to thrive in the competitive realm of AI-driven entrepreneurship.

Building Trust with Customers

Building trust with customers is essential for small businesses and entrepreneurs navigating the competitive landscape of today's market. Trust forms the foundation of customer relationships, influencing their decision-making processes and loyalty. In an increasingly automated world, where technology facilitates interactions, establishing genuine connections becomes even more critical. By leveraging AI-driven tools and personalized approaches, small businesses can cultivate an environment of transparency and reliability that resonates with tech-savvy consumers.

One effective way to build trust is through transparency in communication. AI-driven marketing automation tools can help small businesses maintain consistent and clear messaging across various platforms. By utilizing these tools, entrepreneurs can ensure that their communications are not only timely but also relevant, fostering a sense of reliability. When customers feel informed and engaged, they are more likely to trust the brand and its offerings. Additionally, transparency about pricing, processes, and data usage can significantly enhance customer confidence, particularly in a landscape where privacy concerns are prevalent.

Personalization is another crucial element in establishing trust. Personalized AI recommendations for e-commerce platforms allow businesses to tailor their offerings to individual customer preferences, enhancing the shopping experience. When customers receive suggestions that align with their interests and needs, they feel valued and understood. This tailored approach not only drives sales but also promotes a deeper emotional connection between the customer and the brand. By investing in AI technologies that facilitate personalization, small businesses can create a customer-centric environment that nurtures trust and loyalty.

Moreover, predictive analytics for sales forecasting can play a pivotal role in building trust. By utilizing data-driven insights, entrepreneurs can make informed decisions that resonate with their customers' expectations. This proactive approach demonstrates a commitment to understanding the market and meeting customer needs effectively. When customers recognize that a business is attuned to their preferences and market trends, they are more likely to develop trust in the brand's ability to deliver on its promises. Consistency in quality and service, bolstered by data insights, reinforces this trust over time.

Lastly, the human element cannot be overlooked in the pursuit of building trust. AI solutions for human resources and talent acquisition can enhance the quality of customer interactions by ensuring that businesses hire individuals who embody the brand's values and mission. A well-trained team that understands the importance of customer service and trustworthiness can significantly impact how customers perceive a brand. By marrying technology with a strong human touch, small businesses can create a trustworthy atmosphere that appeals to customers, ultimately leading to sustained growth and loyalty in a competitive market.

Chapter 9: Future Trends in AI for Small Businesses

Emerging AI Technologies and Their Impacts

Emerging AI technologies are rapidly transforming the landscape for small business owners and entrepreneurs, providing innovative solutions that drive growth and efficiency. These advancements are not only enhancing operational processes but also reshaping how businesses engage with their customers. For instance, AI-driven marketing automation tools enable small businesses to tailor their marketing strategies with unprecedented precision, allowing them to deliver personalized content that resonates with target audiences. This shift towards automation not only saves time but also optimizes marketing budgets by ensuring that resources are allocated to the most effective campaigns.

Predictive analytics is another significant development in the AI sphere that is particularly beneficial for small enterprises. By harnessing vast amounts of data, predictive analytics tools can forecast sales trends, enabling businesses to make informed decisions about inventory management, staffing, and product offerings. Small business owners can utilize these insights to anticipate market changes and align their strategies accordingly, thus enhancing their competitive edge. This proactive approach to sales forecasting empowers entrepreneurs to minimize risks and capitalize on emerging opportunities.

In the realm of e-commerce, personalized AI recommendations are revolutionizing customer experiences. These systems analyze user behavior and preferences to suggest products that align with individual tastes, which significantly increases conversion rates. For small e-commerce platforms, this technology not only boosts sales but also fosters customer loyalty, as shoppers are more likely to return to a site that understands and anticipates their needs. As a result, small business owners can leverage AI to create more engaging and relevant shopping experiences, driving repeat business and enhancing overall profitability.

Human resources and talent acquisition are also experiencing significant advancements through AI solutions. Small businesses often face challenges in attracting and retaining top talent due to limited resources. AI-driven platforms streamline the recruitment process by automating candidate screening and matching applicants with job descriptions based on their qualifications and experiences. This not only reduces the time spent on hiring but also helps ensure that small businesses find the right fit for their organizational culture, ultimately contributing to improved employee retention and satisfaction.

Data-driven decision-making tools powered by AI are becoming indispensable for entrepreneurs aiming to navigate the complexities of modern business. These tools enable small business owners to analyze trends, monitor performance, and derive actionable insights from their data. By integrating AI into their decision-making processes, entrepreneurs can enhance their strategic planning, identify areas for improvement, and make informed choices that drive growth. As these emerging technologies continue to evolve, they will undoubtedly provide small businesses with the tools necessary to thrive in an increasingly competitive marketplace.

Preparing for the Future of AI

As small business owners and entrepreneurs navigate the evolving landscape of artificial intelligence, it is crucial to adopt a proactive approach to prepare for its future implications. This preparation involves understanding the fundamental changes AI can bring to various aspects of business operations, including marketing automation, sales forecasting, and human resources. By familiarizing themselves with these technologies, entrepreneurs can position their businesses for growth and efficiency, ultimately enhancing their competitive edge in the marketplace.

One of the most significant areas where AI can transform small businesses is in marketing automation. Entrepreneurs should invest time in exploring AI-driven marketing tools that can personalize customer interactions and streamline campaigns. These tools leverage data to create tailored marketing messages, optimize ad spend, and analyze customer behavior. By embracing these technologies, small business owners can not only improve their customer engagement but also achieve a higher return on investment, making their marketing efforts more effective and efficient.

Moreover, predictive analytics is a game changer for sales forecasting in small enterprises. Entrepreneurs must harness AI's ability to analyze historical data and identify patterns that can inform future business decisions. By utilizing predictive analytics, small businesses can anticipate market trends, optimize inventory levels, and enhance customer segmentation. This forward-thinking approach allows entrepreneurs to make informed decisions based on data-driven insights, reducing the risks associated with uncertainty and fostering sustainable growth.

In the realm of e-commerce, personalized AI recommendations are becoming essential for enhancing the customer experience. Small business owners should focus on implementing AI solutions that analyze customer preferences and behaviors to deliver tailored product suggestions. This personalization not only increases conversion rates but also fosters customer loyalty, as consumers feel understood and valued. Embracing these AI-driven strategies will enable small businesses to compete more effectively with larger enterprises that have already adopted similar technologies.

Finally, AI solutions for human resources and talent acquisition are vital for building a strong workforce. Entrepreneurs should consider AI tools that streamline the hiring process, from candidate sourcing to interview scheduling and performance evaluation. By automating repetitive tasks, small business owners can allocate more time to strategic initiatives that drive growth. Additionally, data-driven decision-making tools powered by AI can offer insights into employee performance and organizational dynamics, enabling entrepreneurs to cultivate a productive and engaged workforce. As AI continues to advance, those who prepare now will be well-equipped to leverage its full potential in the future.

The Role of Entrepreneurs in Shaping AI Developments

Entrepreneurs play a pivotal role in shaping the development and application of artificial intelligence, particularly as it pertains to small businesses. By harnessing AI technologies, these innovators are not just enhancing operational efficiencies; they are redefining industries and creating new market opportunities. The entrepreneurial spirit drives the exploration of AI tools, allowing small businesses to compete with larger corporations by leveraging advanced analytics, machine learning, and automation. This dynamic fosters a culture of innovation that is essential for economic growth and sustainability in the tech-driven marketplace.

In the realm of AI-driven marketing automation, entrepreneurs are utilizing sophisticated algorithms to better understand consumer behavior and preferences. By implementing personalized marketing strategies, small businesses can deliver targeted content and offers, significantly improving customer engagement and conversion rates. The agility of small enterprises allows them to quickly adapt to new AI tools and methodologies, providing them with a competitive edge. As these businesses harness the power of AI, they not only streamline their marketing efforts but also cultivate a more meaningful connection with their customers.

Predictive analytics is another area where entrepreneurs are making significant strides. By utilizing AI to analyze historical data and forecast future trends, small businesses can make informed decisions regarding inventory management, sales strategies, and resource allocation. This data-driven approach minimizes risks associated with uncertainty and enhances the overall strategic planning process. Entrepreneurs who embrace predictive analytics are better positioned to identify market opportunities and respond proactively to shifting consumer demands, thereby driving growth and profitability.

E-commerce platforms also benefit tremendously from the entrepreneurial application of AI. Personalized recommendations powered by AI algorithms enhance the shopping experience by providing consumers with tailored product suggestions based on their browsing and purchasing histories. Small businesses that implement these AI solutions can compete more effectively in the crowded online marketplace. By offering a customized shopping experience, entrepreneurs can not only increase sales but also build brand loyalty, positioning their businesses for long-term success in an ever-evolving digital landscape.

Lastly, AI solutions for human resources and talent acquisition are transforming the way small businesses manage their workforce. Entrepreneurs are leveraging AI-driven tools to streamline recruitment processes, improve employee engagement, and enhance overall productivity. By utilizing data analytics to identify the best candidates and assess employee performance, small business owners can make more informed hiring decisions and foster a positive work environment. This strategic application of AI not only optimizes human resources but also empowers entrepreneurs to build resilient teams capable of navigating the complexities of the modern business world.

Conclusion: Embracing the AI Revolution

The AI revolution presents an unprecedented opportunity for small business owners and entrepreneurs to transform their operations and enhance their competitive edge. As advancements in artificial intelligence continue to reshape various industries, embracing these technologies is no longer optional but essential for survival and growth. By integrating AI-driven solutions, small enterprises can streamline processes, improve decision-making, and ultimately drive profitability. This chapter highlights the importance of adopting AI tools and technologies to stay ahead in a rapidly evolving marketplace.

One of the most significant advantages of AI for small businesses lies in its ability to automate marketing efforts. AI-driven marketing automation tools enable entrepreneurs to optimize their outreach strategies, target the right audience, and personalize customer interactions. This not only enhances customer engagement but also increases conversion rates. By leveraging data analytics, small businesses can gain valuable insights into consumer behavior, allowing them to craft tailored marketing campaigns that resonate with their target demographic.

In addition to marketing, predictive analytics plays a crucial role in sales forecasting for small enterprises. By utilizing AI algorithms to analyze historical data and market trends, businesses can make informed predictions about future sales performance. This predictive capability empowers entrepreneurs to allocate resources more effectively, manage inventory, and adjust their strategies based on real-time insights. Embracing predictive analytics fosters a proactive approach to business management, enabling small enterprises to navigate challenges and seize opportunities with confidence.

E-commerce platforms also stand to benefit significantly from personalized AI recommendations. By implementing AI algorithms, businesses can enhance the shopping experience by providing tailored product suggestions based on individual customer preferences and purchase history. This not only improves customer satisfaction but also drives sales by encouraging repeat purchases. As consumers increasingly expect personalized experiences, leveraging AI for recommendation systems is essential for maintaining competitiveness in the e-commerce space.

Finally, AI solutions for human resources and talent acquisition are revolutionizing the way small businesses manage their workforce. From automating candidate screening processes to predicting employee performance, AI can streamline HR functions and improve hiring outcomes. Additionally, data-driven decision-making tools empower entrepreneurs to analyze employee data and identify patterns that contribute to a more effective and engaged workforce. By embracing AI in human resources, small business owners can foster a culture of innovation and adaptability, positioning themselves for sustained growth in an ever-changing business landscape.

Chapter 10: Resources and Tools for the AI Entrepreneur

Recommended AI Tools and Software

In today's rapidly evolving business landscape, small business owners and entrepreneurs must harness the power of artificial intelligence to remain competitive and drive growth. A variety of AI tools and software have emerged, specifically designed to cater to the unique needs of small enterprises. These resources not only streamline operations but also enhance decision-making processes through data-driven insights. This subchapter highlights some of the most recommended AI tools that can empower entrepreneurs to optimize their strategies and achieve sustainable success.

For marketing automation, platforms like HubSpot and Mailchimp stand out as essential tools for small businesses. These solutions leverage AI to analyze customer behavior and preferences, enabling entrepreneurs to create highly targeted marketing campaigns. With features such as predictive analytics, these tools can forecast customer engagement and optimize email marketing efforts, ensuring that messages resonate with the intended audience. By automating repetitive tasks, business owners can focus on higher-level strategy and creative initiatives, ultimately driving growth and fostering customer loyalty.

When it comes to sales forecasting, AI-driven platforms like Salesforce Einstein and Zoho CRM offer invaluable insights for small enterprises. These tools analyze historical data and current market trends to deliver accurate predictions regarding sales performance. By utilizing predictive analytics, entrepreneurs can make informed decisions about inventory management, staffing, and marketing budgets. The ability to anticipate sales fluctuations allows business owners to allocate resources more effectively, ensuring resilience in an ever-changing marketplace.

E-commerce platforms are increasingly incorporating personalized AI recommendations to enhance the customer shopping experience. Tools such as Dynamic Yield and Nosto provide small businesses with the ability to deliver tailored product suggestions based on individual user behavior and preferences. This personalization not only increases conversion rates but also fosters customer satisfaction and loyalty. By leveraging AI to curate unique shopping experiences, entrepreneurs can differentiate their brand in a crowded marketplace and drive repeat business.

Human resources and talent acquisition are also being transformed by AI solutions. Tools like BambooHR and HireVue utilize AI to streamline recruitment processes, from candidate sourcing to interview scheduling. These platforms employ machine learning algorithms to identify top candidates based on specific criteria, significantly reducing the time and effort involved in hiring. Additionally, AI-driven performance management tools can help entrepreneurs assess employee productivity and engagement, enabling data-driven decisions that enhance organizational culture and workforce effectiveness. By integrating AI into HR practices, small business owners can build strong teams that drive their companies forward.

Online Courses and Learning Resources

Online courses and learning resources have become critical components in the toolkit of today's entrepreneurs, especially for those navigating the rapidly evolving landscape of artificial intelligence. The accessibility of these resources allows small business owners and tech-curious individuals to enhance their skills and knowledge at their own pace. Platforms such as Coursera, Udacity, and edX offer a wealth of courses specifically tailored to AI applications in business, marketing, and analytics. These courses often feature industry leaders and practitioners as instructors, providing valuable insights and real-world applications that can be directly implemented in small business operations.

In the realm of AI-driven marketing automation, specialized online courses equip entrepreneurs with the tools necessary to optimize their marketing strategies. These courses cover topics such as customer segmentation, campaign management, and performance tracking using AI technologies. By understanding these concepts, small business owners can harness the power of AI to create personalized marketing experiences that resonate with their target audience, ultimately driving higher engagement and conversion rates. Furthermore, many platforms offer certifications that can enhance credibility and demonstrate expertise to potential clients and partners.

Predictive analytics is another area where online learning resources shine. Courses focused on data analytics teach entrepreneurs how to leverage AI to forecast sales and understand market trends. By employing predictive models, small business owners can make informed decisions about inventory management, product development, and resource allocation. The ability to anticipate customer needs and market fluctuations can significantly enhance a business's competitiveness and profitability. Engaging with these courses not only fosters a deeper understanding of analytics but also cultivates a data-driven culture within the organization.

E-commerce platforms are increasingly integrating personalized AI recommendations to improve customer experiences and drive sales. Online courses dedicated to this subject provide entrepreneurs with insights into machine learning algorithms and recommendation systems. Understanding how to implement these technologies allows small business owners to tailor their offerings to individual customer preferences, thereby increasing customer satisfaction and loyalty. Resources that focus on the practical application of AI in e-commerce empower entrepreneurs to stay ahead of the curve and meet the demands of today's consumers.

Finally, the importance of AI solutions in human resources and talent acquisition cannot be overlooked. Online learning platforms frequently offer courses that cover AI-driven recruitment tools, employee engagement strategies, and performance analytics. Small business owners can learn to utilize these innovations to streamline their hiring processes, improve employee retention, and foster a more dynamic workplace culture. By embracing AI in human resources, entrepreneurs can optimize their talent management strategies, ultimately leading to a more effective and motivated workforce. Investing time in these educational resources is essential for entrepreneurs seeking to leverage AI for sustainable growth and efficiency in their businesses.

Networking and Community Support

Networking and community support are crucial elements for success in the entrepreneurial landscape, especially for those venturing into the realm of artificial intelligence. As small business owners and tech-curious millennials explore AI-driven solutions, connecting with like-minded individuals and organizations can foster innovation and collaboration. Establishing a robust network allows entrepreneurs to share insights, resources, and experiences, ultimately leading to more informed decisions and enhanced growth opportunities.

Engaging with local and online communities dedicated to AI and entrepreneurship can provide invaluable support. Many platforms host forums, webinars, and workshops where entrepreneurs can learn from industry experts and peers. These interactions not only broaden knowledge about AI-driven marketing automation tools and predictive analytics for sales forecasting but also facilitate the exchange of best practices. Such environments are ideal for cultivating relationships that may lead to partnerships, mentorship, and even potential clients.

Another significant advantage of networking is the ability to stay abreast of the latest trends and technologies in AI. By attending industry conferences, participating in online meetups, and joining relevant social media groups, entrepreneurs can gain insights into emerging tools and strategies. For instance, understanding advancements in personalized AI recommendations for e-commerce platforms can empower small businesses to enhance customer experiences and drive sales. Staying connected with the community ensures that entrepreneurs are not left behind in a rapidly evolving technological landscape.

Moreover, community support can often translate into collaborative opportunities. Entrepreneurs can find partners to co-develop AI solutions for human resources and talent acquisition or engage in joint marketing initiatives. These collaborations can lead to cost savings and improved service offerings, enhancing competitive advantages. By leveraging collective expertise and resources, entrepreneurs can navigate challenges more effectively and drive innovation within their businesses.

In conclusion, networking and community support play a pivotal role in the journey of AI entrepreneurs. By building strong connections, staying informed about industry advancements, and exploring collaborative opportunities, small business owners can unlock the full potential of AI technologies. Embracing these elements not only enriches their entrepreneurial experience but also positions them for sustainable growth and success in an increasingly digital world.

Final Thoughts and Next Steps

As we reach the conclusion of this exploration into the intersection of artificial intelligence and entrepreneurship, it is essential to reflect on the transformative potential that these technologies hold for small business owners. The integration of AI-driven tools can significantly streamline operations, enhance marketing efforts, and improve decision-making processes. By leveraging predictive analytics and personalized recommendations, entrepreneurs can better understand their customers, forecast sales more accurately, and ultimately drive growth in ways that were previously unimaginable. The future of entrepreneurship is undoubtedly intertwined with these technological advancements, and those who adapt will thrive.

Moving forward, entrepreneurs should prioritize the identification and implementation of AI tools that align with their specific business needs. Whether it's adopting marketing automation platforms to enhance customer engagement or utilizing predictive analytics for more informed sales strategies, the focus should be on tools that offer tangible benefits. Investing time in understanding the capabilities of various AI solutions will empower business owners to make informed decisions that can lead to sustained growth and efficiency. This proactive approach will not only enhance operational effectiveness but also position businesses to stay competitive in an increasingly digital marketplace.

Moreover, small business owners should consider fostering a culture of innovation within their organizations. Embracing AI is not merely about technology; it involves a mindset shift that encourages experimentation and adaptation. Training staff to utilize new tools and fostering collaboration between teams can maximize the benefits of AI. As employees become more comfortable with these technologies, they can contribute insights that lead to further optimization of processes and improved customer experiences. This cultural shift will be crucial in ensuring that businesses fully harness the potential of AI.

Networking and seeking mentorship within the entrepreneurial community can also provide valuable insights into best practices for AI implementation. Engaging with peers who have successfully integrated AI into their operations can offer practical guidance and inspiration. Additionally, many organizations and platforms are dedicated to supporting entrepreneurs in navigating the complexities of AI technology. Leveraging these resources can help demystify the process and provide a clearer pathway for small business owners looking to embark on their AI journey.

In conclusion, the integration of AI tools into small businesses represents a significant opportunity for growth and efficiency. By remaining informed, fostering a culture of innovation, and connecting with the broader entrepreneurial ecosystem, small business owners can position themselves at the forefront of this technological evolution. The steps taken today will pave the way for a more resilient and competitive future, where AI serves as an invaluable ally in the quest for business success. Embracing these next steps will not only enhance individual enterprises but also contribute to a broader movement towards a more data-driven and intelligent approach to entrepreneurship.

www.ingramcontent.com/pod-product-compliance
Lightning Source LLC
Chambersburg PA
CBHW070408230526
45471CB00006B/2702